Motivating Students Who Don't Care

Successful Techniques for Educators

Allen N. Mendler

National Educational Service

Cover art and design by Grannan Graphic Design Ltd.

Text design by T.G. Design Group

Art by Randi Moody

Printed in the United States of America

ISBN 1-879639-81-5

Dedication

To my wonderful daughter Lisa, whose goodness, caring, and enthusiasm for life inspires me to keep working at making our schools places of success for all students.

To Brian, my bright and sensitive son, whose remarkable resilience is testament that struggles in and out of school can build character and success with the support of caring adults.

To Ticia, my daughter-in-law, who is testament to how effort and balance make for success.

To my son Jason, whose inner tenacity, self-motivation, and love of learning reminds me of the influence that educators who enthusiastically convey their knowledge can have on their students.

Acknowledgments

I WISH TO THANK THE MANY EDUCATORS around the country who appreciate my work and share their work with me. They inspire me to create, implement, and then offer practical ideas that make a difference for students.

Special thanks is given to Rick Curwin, my partner, best friend, and frequent co-author, for contributing some of this material which is contained in our book, *Discipline with Dignity for Challenging Youth* (Mendler & Curwin, 1999).

In addition, I want to thank the following people whose ongoing support is most appreciated:

- Tammy Rowland, my program and office manager at Discipline Associates

- Phil Harris at the Association for Educational Communications and Technology

- Jeff Jones at the National Educational Service

- Frank Koontz at the Bureau of Education and Research

- Nancy Modrak at the Association for Supervision and Curriculum Development

- MaryAnn Beiter at the Learning Institute

- Larry Brendtro at Reclaiming Youth International

- Leah Jerabek at the Milwaukee Public Schools

- Laura McCullough at the Kentucky Department of Education

- Dave and Colleen Zawadzki at Syracuse City Schools

- Elizabeth Oster at the Rochester City Schools

Finally, as always, a special thank-you to my wife, Barbara, for her love and intimacy.

Table of Contents

Introduction

"I don't have to if I don't want to!"

"This class is boring."

"When am I ever going to use that!"

"How come you gave me an F?"

"I'll come, but you can't make me do anything."

MORE TEACHERS THAN EVER are frustrated with legions of students who expect success but are unwilling to work for it. "Fast and easy" has replaced "work and earn" as a motto that guides too many of our youth. Students are missing the idea that it is their responsibility to learn information, practice material, and attend school. They often feel as though they should be adequately entertained. Feeling good has become more valued than working hard. Students of today are much like the character in the comic strip "The Wizard of Id." The character applies for a job and is asked, "Do you have any education?" He answers, "No, but I have high self-esteem." Expectations of entitlement with minimal effort are not uncommon in today's classrooms.

There is a direct relationship between motivation and discipline. The hard to motivate are often hard to discipline. Our seminars are increasingly attended by educators who question what to do with students who are not prepared, do not care, and will not work, although it is difficult to assess which is the cause and which is the result. Finding tools and strategies to increase motivation can solve many behavior problems. Although these problems defy simplistic solutions, there are many things that educators can do to reawaken motivation in students who have lost interest and perhaps hope. Those who are hard to motivate and control often make us wonder why we should bother with them at all when there are so many others who care and want to learn. They make us question the worth of reaching out to them when they often sap our own energy and motivation. In addition, they often push our buttons, make us feel defeated, interfere with other students, challenge our authority, and evoke strong emotions that interfere with reason. Unless we are careful, they can burn us out.

Chapter 1

Why Are Students Unmotivated?

AN EXPECTATION OF ENTITLEMENT is easy to acquire in a culture that too often values what we have rather than who we are. During an age in which abundance of things seems to take precedence over giving the gift of our time, guilt often leads parents to give materially to their children without attaching expectations. When children are spoiled into believing that what they want is what they should have, school provides a rude awakening when it links success to personal effort. Changing the culture is difficult at best, so wise educators need to understand and use social dynamics to create, inspire, and cultivate motivation within their students.

From a psychological perspective, many students who have bad behavior or who give up are covering their concerns about being perceived as stupid. They are protecting themselves from the embarrassment of looking dumb in the eyes of their classmates, parents, and selves. Some students find power and control in their refusals to work. They are often competent and capable, but their need to be in control is so strong that they employ a self-defeating strategy to exert their independence. Depression among children as young as preschoolers is often overlooked as a cause of poor school motivation. When depression is adequately diagnosed, treatment through counseling and drug therapy can often be effective. Whether for competence or autonomy, lack of motivation is a protective mechanism that must be respectfully challenged in order to help students make better choices.

Our professional responsibility requires that we teach all students and make our best effort to excite even those who seem not to care. If we give up on them, they will cause more problems and be more hurtful, dangerous, and costly. Just as a good subject area curriculum provides the big picture along with specific units of instruction, this book offers a curriculum guide along with many specific methods that can help us motivate students who don't care.

Chapter 2

Using This Book Most Effectively

ALL OF THE STRATEGIES THAT ARE OFFERED in this book have proven themselves to be very effective tools in motivating students. Although the goal of this book is to offer educators specific, practical, and proven strategies, it is not a cookbook with the recipe for producing perfectly motivated students. Instead, it offers a set of beliefs followed by five specific processes that form the framework for the many classroom-friendly strategies designed to inspire motivation in students who are giving up. It is most important to be guided by the framework rather than to feel compelled to use all of the strategies.

Although the book can be viewed as a comprehensive and practical guide, my hope is that you will employ the strategies that will work best for you while using the framework to invent new strategies as needed. Some strategies conclude with a suggestion section. This section offers specific ways that the suggestion can be implemented. Those strategies that do not contain a suggestion section are viewed as sufficiently obvious to be implemented without further information.

Chapter 3

What Educators Can Do: Five Key Processes That Motivate

BEING SUCCESSFUL AT MOTIVATING DIFFICULT YOUTH requires that our behavior be motivated by the following basic beliefs:

1. All students are capable of learning when they have the academic and personal tools to be successful.

2. Students are inherently motivated to learn but learn to be unmotivated when they repeatedly fail.

3. Learning requires risk taking, so classrooms need to be safe places physically and psychologically.

4. All students have basic needs to belong, to be competent, and to influence what happens to them. Motivation to learn most often occurs when these basic needs are met.

5. High self-esteem should not be a goal, but rather a result that comes with the mastery of challenging tasks.

6. High motivation for learning in school most often occurs when adults treat students with respect and dignity.

These tenets are driven by the following five key processes that educators can use for guidance as they apply or create strategies that inspire and reinforce:

- Emphasizing effort
- Creating hope
- Respecting power
- Building relationships
- Expressing enthusiasm

These processes will be discussed in the five chapters that follow, with a description of what each process involves and specific strategies for introducing the process into your own school or classroom.

Chapter 4

Emphasizing Effort

PUTTING THE FOCUS ON EFFORT IS CRUCIAL to increasing achievement, promoting learning, and minimizing behavior problems among students who are hiding their academic inadequacies. Most students who present themselves unfavorably, whether through their lack of motivation or their inappropriate behavior, are trying to conceal their concerns about academic or performance inadequacy. In a nutshell, they simply do not see themselves as capable and usually attribute success to ability rather than effort. As Carol Dweck's research has shown, these students believe that intelligence is a fixed entity and is the factor responsible for success or failure (cited in Azar, 1996). By contrast, successful learners generally believe that their effort is the key factor in determining success. The end result is that many students who fail simply do not try because they believe that even if they worked harder, their achievement still would not improve in any substantial way. Although it is difficult to get such students to put forth greater effort, there are many classroom techniques that can work when the emphasis is placed on the relationship between achievement and effort.

Build on Mistakes or Partially Correct Answers

Mistakes are potent learning tools when viewed diagnostically rather than evaluatively. In school, teachers can build on mistakes to increase learning when we frame them as part of the instruction process rather than as an indication of failure. Leading educator Madeline Hunter suggested that wrong answers be dignified by acknowledging the part that is right. For example, "Lincoln wasn't the first, but you're right about his being president," or "Juan, you did a great job on four of your answers. They show that you understand the first part of the story. Look over my suggestions on the next four, and see how that can make your essay even stronger."

In discussions and classroom projects, mistakes can be used to highlight how more teaching still needs to occur and/or how learning processes need to be improved. For example, "Heather, your mistake helps me understand that I need to explain this concept more clearly. I bet others were also confused. Thanks for the help." Appreciating effort is the first step toward improvement.

Suggestion. Children are always told that it is okay to make mistakes because that is how they learn. Yet we often reward only the best answers or performances. If we want students to really believe that we are encouraging them to learn from their mistakes, then we need to actually point out the benefits when we see them. Get in the habit of explaining what mistakes teach. Here is a suggested sequence for explanation:

1. You (student) show a really good understanding of

    _____.

    (Begin with a strength based upon an aspect of the student's work that showed the kind of thinking you were looking for.)

2. Your mistake is a good reminder to _____.
   (Give explanation or new information that helps pro-
   mote understanding beyond the mistake.)

3. Now that you seem to understand even better, I'd like
   you to do one or two more for practice. (Give specific
   practice problems.)

4. Offer congratulations when improvement is shown.

Allow the 3 Rs—Redo, Retake, and Revise

Rarely is the first attempt a final endeavor. Writers usually edit
several drafts before submission. Architects carefully review and
revise a design for a bridge before building begins. Accountants go
over their books carefully. Improvement is a sure sign of effort.
Although effort is hard to measure, a separate grade for effort rein-
forces the importance of working to one's capacity. Obviously, an
increase in test scores demonstrates improvement and can be used
as an indicator of effort. In addition, you might brainstorm with
your class for other indicators that show your students how
important improvement is to you.

It is unrealistic to expect students to do their best work on a
one-time-only basis. Allowing students to retake tests and revise
projects, papers, and experiments in response to feedback from
the teacher or other students enhances effort and learning.
Although curriculum modifications are sometimes appropriate,
simply adding the redo, retake, or revise option lets students know
that their effort can lead to improved achievement.

Naturally, there must be a proper balance for students between
opportunities to improve their performance and demonstrating
responsibility. Teachers should inform students about what they

need to do to improve and how long they have to work on improving the product. For example, a semester's worth of papers should not be accepted one day before grades are due. Care also must be taken to avoid promoting procrastination and minimal effort on the first attempts.

Suggestion. To encourage early effort, you might allow students to accumulate points in a "bank account" for early, outstanding production of assignments. These points can be exchanged for an excused homework or test when sufficient points have accumulated. Another option is to give slightly lower weighting to improved assignments than to on-time, first-time efforts. For example, if a student's first test score is 50% and the next is 80%, there can be a 20% deduction between the original and the make-up. (In this case, the difference between the first and second is 30 points times 20% = 6 points.) The student's score would then be 74%. You can also brainstorm other ideas for identifying improvement with colleagues and/or your students.

Separate Effort From Achievement When Grading

Grades cannot adequately provide a comprehensive picture of performance because we try to cover too many variables in a grade (Marzano, 2000). Grades can be far more effective and gain motivational value when we separate what we evaluate by category. Students are more likely to become or remain motivated when their strengths are acknowledged while their needs are addressed.

Two separate grades can be given: one for achievement and the other for effort. For example, the achievement grade represents the degree of subject mastery demonstrated by outcome measures such as performance on a unit test, production of a portfolio, or comprehensive treatment of subject matter. It seeks to assess *what* the student learns. The effort grade is earned for *how* the student performs while learning and is based on such factors as participation and homework. Because the primary goal of grading in an educational setting is to provide feedback that summarizes a student's strengths and needs, a two-category system is better able to offer comprehensive feedback.

Suggestion. Make a list of all the factors you use to determine a student's grade. After you have listed all of these factors, ask yourself which of these measures focus on what a student has learned and which focus more on how the student performs or behaves while learning. You can use the items listed under *what* to establish an achievement grade and those under *how* as an effort grade.

Encourage Each Student to Improve One Little Thing Every Day

Have each student identify one small thing to do each day (academically, socially, or emotionally) that will either help the student become better at something or make the world a better place. Examples are doing one more math problem, ignoring a challenge to fight, or giving a friendly greeting to a person you do not normally talk to. Keeping an improvement log that tracks progress can be helpful.

Show Simple Courtesy

Sadly, it seems that too many of us are so preoccupied with our own lives that we neglect to consider the impact that small moments of courtesy can have upon others. When a student turns in an assignment or takes a test, give feedback promptly. Not doing so makes the feedback far less meaningful. In fact, making students wait more than 3 days for feedback negates its valuable effect on learning. But even if learning would still occur, common courtesy would suggest promptness. If a friend asked us to read something of his or hers, would we not want to offer our input promptly? Do we not appreciate those people who return our calls or answer our questions promptly, but experience anger toward those who treat us with indifference?

To illustrate the impact of courtesy, a story involving one of my sons comes to mind. He is a young, self-motivated sportscaster who wants to move ahead in an extremely competitive field. Job postings often yield hundreds of applicants who send in their résumé tapes hoping that someone will bother to look at the tape and request an interview. The applicant pays all expenses for résumé tapes and travel for an interview. My son has been a finalist a few times, but has yet to be chosen for a highly prized position. Although he is disappointed when he does not get the job, the most frustrating part of the process for him is the lack of common courtesy. His energy, motivation, and self-confidence are slowly being sapped when he does not receive a thank-you letter for applying and often driving long distances at his own expense or a simple phone call of appreciation with the message that he was not the first choice. It is so very important to remember that our thoughtfulness can be a major tool in both inspiring and sustaining the motivation of others.

> **Suggestion.** Think about all of the small gestures of courtesy that you value and appreciate. Perhaps you find it valuable when your principal offers a kind word or a parent calls in appreciation of something you have done for her child. Maybe it is a simple thank-you given to you by either a student or an administrator. Make a point of offering thoughtful, simple courtesies to your students and watch their motivation increase—they will want to be around you.

Reframe Unmotivated Behavior to Encourage Effort

We have a much better chance of getting effort from the unmotivated when we let the student know that she is more important than what she does. Although behavior has consequences, student motivation increases when students know that we care more about them than about what they do. A shift in our thinking will often lead to more influential behavior. The challenge is identifying and communicating the positive aspects of what the student's behavior represents while encouraging more of the same. For example, if a student turns in a homework assignment with 2 questions attempted or completed out of 10, can we focus more on the 2 done than on the 8 that were not done? We can say, "Jason, these two were done very well. Congratulations. Tell me how you approached these and what you did that made you so successful. If you did the others, how could you use the skills you already have?"

Can we allow ourselves to realize that a student who chronically comes 5 minutes late for a 50-minute class is present 90% of the time, which would be an A or A- on any other graded measure of achievement? Seeing it this way would enable us to affirm the student and give a consequence. For example,

> Ann, I'll probably keep hassling you to get here on time, but when I think about it, you're here for most of the class. I miss you when you're not here, which is why I hassle you. Even when you aren't interested in class, you're important to me because I sometimes get the idea that maybe you're not the only bored student. So if you can find a way to get here on time, I'd love to see you. If not, and the best I can get is 5 minutes late, then I guess I'll need to live with that. Either way, keep coming.

The communication can end with a consequence when appropriate (e.g., "Ann, here is today's late referral").

Suggestion. Find something positive to share with a student who is poorly motivated before focusing on the consequences. For example, after a student has gotten a failing grade on a test, respond by saying, "Lamar, you showed up and took the test, which I know took effort. I'm convinced that more effort in studying before you come to take the next test will lead to a better grade next time."

Ask for Small Things First

People tend to act in accordance with how they view themselves. So if you want a student to comply with your request to do something, you stand a much better chance of eliciting compliance by asking for just a little bit more each time and building the request upon what has been done previously. For example, "Sam, I enjoyed hearing your idea in class today. You seem to have a lot of ideas about many things, and I appreciate when you share a few of them in class."

> Suggestion. Focus and build on small successes. Identify behaviors that you want the student to show more frequently (e.g., I want Sam to _____ more often). When you see evidence of these positive behaviors, notice and be appreciative.

Put the Effort in Writing so That It Becomes a Commitment

There is much research that shows a strong deepening of commitment and follow-through when goals, promises, and plans are written. It is not accidental that most contracts are put in writing and signed by those who agree to their terms.

> **Suggestion.** You might develop some simple forms and have students use these to share the key details of commitments they make (see Table 1). Another option is to thank students for all of their ideas for increasing effort. Ask students to write these down so that you will be able to correctly remember what has been agreed upon.

Table 1

CONTRACT FOR INCREASING COMMITMENT

1. What can you do to be more successful at school?
   _____
   _____

2. What is your plan for making more of an effort to be more successful?_____
   _____

3. What obstacles or difficulties might keep you from making your plan a success?
   _____
   _____

4. What are some ways you can stay away from these obstacles or overcome them if they occur?
   _____
   _____

5. How can I or other people at school help you be successful with your plan?
   _____
   _____

6. What are some fair consequences that you should face if your plan does not work?
   _____
   _____

_____   _____
(student's signature)   (teacher's signature)

Give a Reason for Effort

A well-known principle of human behavior is that when we ask someone to do us a favor, we will be more successful if we provide a reason. Social psychologist Ellen Langer (1989) demonstrated this in a simple experiment by asking a small favor of people waiting in line to use a library copying machine. When she asked them to move ahead without a reason by saying, "Excuse me, I have five pages. May I use the Xerox machine?" 60% complied. When she offered a reason and said, "Excuse me, I have five pages. May I use the Xerox machine because I'm in a rush?" 94% let her slip ahead. Of even greater interest is that even without a good reason, when she stated, "Excuse me, I have five pages. May I use the Xerox machine because I have to make some copies?" 93% complied. These results imply that if we provide a reason to students for why we make requests or demands, they are much more likely to comply even when the reason does not make much sense. Realize that providing an answer to the question why, which is often what students are wondering, strengthens the effectiveness of telling them what to do and how to do it.

> **Suggestion.** Make a list of daily classroom obligations (e.g., assignments, homework, classwork, and class routines). Practice giving these while providing a reason ("Do at least five multiplication problems because that is the fewest number for practice that really makes us remember how to solve these problems").

Celebrate Markers and Endings

Encourage individual and group celebrations for the achievement of identified goals. For example, "Mark, Quan, Cabil, and Keisha now know their five times tables. Let's applaud them." It can help to congratulate groups or the class when an ending has been achieved: "Whew, that was a tough unit on molecules. I've brought in some molecular apple pie to help us celebrate getting through it."

Questions for Reflection

1. Why do you think many kids change from being very enthusiastic and excited about attending school in the early grades to becoming poorly motivated as they get older?

2. For your students who appear unmotivated in class, what do you believe motivates them in other places in their lives? If you are unsure, you might want to check with them to explore whether any of what motivates them elsewhere might be applicable within the class.

3. When you are faced with challenges in your life, what do you usually do to muster up the effort to get the job done?

Chapter 5

Creating Hope

STUDENTS WHO BELIEVE THEY CANNOT MASTER the curriculum or that mastery will not improve their lives in a meaningful way are the least motivated of all and the most likely to develop behavior problems. Finding the right level of challenge is one of the most important tasks we face in reaching students. Csikszentmihalyi (1990) has demonstrated that when the level of challenge is too low, motivation is lost. Climbing a mound of dirt cannot motivate the same way that climbing a mountain can. Tasks that are too easy are not beneficial. And if a student fails at an easy task, the results are significantly more harmful because the student concludes, "I'm stupid." When tasks are too difficult, students give up.

Our challenge, then, is to create mountains that students believe they can climb. View each classroom and subject as a mountain chain with peaks of different heights, and try to ensure a match between the peak and the aptitude of the climber. When challenge matches ability, the conditions are right for students to participate with enthusiasm.

In truth, children and teenagers learn to be unmotivated. All healthy infants are born inquisitive, curious, and motivated.

Those who remain healthy grow to be toddlers who are so motivated that their parents have to rearrange their homes by erecting gates and blocking steps. Even sick infants who survive are motivated by the life force of survival. Our interests and talents need nurturing if they are to bloom. These dynamics are the foundation of effective conventional and unconventional interventions that build hope and increase motivation.

Show How Achievement Benefits Their Lives

Showing how achievement benefits students' lives is the most conventional way of inspiring motivation. Get a good education, we say, get a good job, make money, and have a good life. Although some students will not want to believe this—they know that good things that should happen do not always happen—the reality is that most college graduates do better financially than high school graduates, who do better than high school dropouts. Therefore, we need to continue using data like these as a tool.

In addition, students who are not obedience oriented and who do not necessarily trust those in authority need to see the connection between what we teach them and how it relates to their lives. They need to see how explorers such as Balboa are still relevant today and how solving an equation in a math class today may relate to the basketball shot they choose to take tomorrow and the car they drive or the house they live in later on.

Finally, showing how achievement benefits their lives can help students when they observe and experience people they can relate to doing things in their lives that use the information presented. Effective mentoring programs bring successful people into school and arrange for them to connect with students in the workplace so youth can see that the benefits of achievement are real. As

Tomlinson (2000) notes, "students will learn best when they can make a connection between the curriculum and their interests and life experiences."

It is important to remember that students view time differently than adults do. This can make conventional methods of motivation less effective. It is not unusual for high school students to see the future as within a month, middle school students as 2 weeks, and elementary students as 3 days. Teachers who can find benefits for the students within these time frames can increase hope. Finding these benefits depends on knowing the students and their true aspirations beyond the obvious ones such as good careers or making money. Benefits need to fit in with students' lifestyles and environment, not to concede to them but to expand from a base of reality.

One potential benefit for all students can be the joy and love their teachers have for what they teach. Continuously demonstrate with words, actions, body language, and emotion why you love what you are teaching by first identifying it and then communicating it. If you do not love what you teach, you will communicate that to your students. Find at least something to love within the subject or choose not to teach it.

Ensure Adequacy of Basic Skills

Students must have basic reading, writing, math, and listening skills. There is simply no substitute. Without these skills, there is no amount of support, praise, or encouragement that will sustain learning. The use of any ethical behavior that persuades students to acquire these skills is suggested. There are times when forceful yet dignified confrontation is needed. Refusals to try can be linked to fear, whereas efforts to achieve should be connected to heroism.

The reality is that many students who lack hope for success believe that they are stupid and incapable. This belief must be strongly challenged. The teacher might confront the student in this way:

> Juran, students who don't work and won't try are usually afraid to fail. It's interesting that even though you try to come across as a tough guy, we both know that underneath, you're scared. Doing nothing, like you do, is the safe play. It is what people who are scared do. I can understand that. Sometimes I play it that way, too. It takes guts and courage to try, especially when there is no guarantee that things will work out. I know that once you get going and attack these math problems with the same force that you use to stick up for yourself, you'll feel proud. I look forward to seeing your effort.

> **Suggestion.** When the student either makes or does not make the effort, connect that back to this theme. You can also apply this method with groups of students who show hopelessness and refuse to try.

Create Challenges That Can Be Mastered

In our seminars, we often challenge participants to find a partner and together count the number of times the letter "e" appears on a U.S. penny. We give them 1 minute to complete the exercise. At least 95% do the task, and when we call time, several continue beyond the time allotted. We remind them that they are actually cheating when they keep going after we have told them to stop. Naturally, most participants are interested in the official answer, so when we tell them that we do not know the answer because we have never done the task, many groan as if realizing they have been had. Although there is a certain satisfaction for us in this harmless fun, the main point made is that we motivated a very large group of intelligent, well-educated professionals to do a meaningless task. This was accomplished by giving them an unusual task with a reasonable challenge that could be successfully achieved in a sensible period of time. Educators can often inspire motivation by varying the type of instruction while providing tasks with identifiable outcomes that can be achieved within a reasonable time.

Acknowledge Your Mistakes

We sometimes fail to realize the power of hope that can be conveyed when someone who is successful makes mistakes, acknowledges those mistakes, and shows what they have learned. If students point out an error you have made in your instruction, thank them for noticing. If you have been abrupt with a student, apologize. Find opportunities to share your less-than-perfect side with your students. They will appreciate you more, as you are living proof that success comes from learning from the mistakes you make.

Help Students Develop Goals

Motivation is facilitated when students create attainable goals that are specific. Ideally, these goals should be measurable and observable to the student. Six specific steps are usually helpful to students in developing effective goals:

1. Decide on a goal that you want to reach.

2. Decide on a plan to attain this goal. What are the steps you need to take and in which order should they be taken?

3. Decide on a reward that you will give yourself when you achieve your goal. You can also give yourself smaller rewards after you achieve one or a few steps in your plan.

4. Check your plan with a parent, teacher, or trusted friend.

5. Do each step in your plan, one at a time.

6. Reward yourself when you have reached your goal.

Help Students Get and Stay Organized

Because school requires that students master a predetermined body of information that may or may not actually interest them, getting and staying organized is essential for success. Unfortunately, many students live relatively disorganized lives outside of school and have not learned how to organize themselves or their materials in ways that are compatible with success. When students are prepared for learning with proper supplies and can anticipate upcoming activities, their chances for success dramatically improve. With students who lack motivation, the wise teacher picks her battles wisely. It is best to avoid hassles over whether a student has necessary supplies until after the student experiences success. Poorly motivated students are best given dessert (to excite their learning) before they are expected to eat their meat and potatoes (assume responsibility for the details).

> **Suggestion.** Many students, particularly those with attention deficit/hyperactivity disorder, have great difficulty anticipating upcoming events and tend to have trouble behaving during transitions. Younger children can benefit from a picture schedule or photos of upcoming activities, and older students can benefit from a checklist of the day's schedule. Another option is to provide a daily or weekly assignment sheet for students and their parents. It is often best to mail home a copy of the assignment sheet to parents and ask that they acknowledge receiving it. Finally, encourage students to keep a different-colored folder for each subject. The folder can be further organized to define specific tasks.

Collect Supplies From Students

Problems in the classroom can often become opportunities. Classroom community building can actually be promoted because of unprepared students. When being prepared is viewed as a strength, then those who are prepared can help others who are not. Rather than have a power struggle with students over issues of preparedness, encourage all students to contribute supplies as needed. With an abundance of necessary supplies contributed by peers, a student's forgetful behavior can become an opportunity for him to simply get the needed material, taking little or no time away from learning. The teacher can ask students to donate pencils, extra notebooks, and other supplies as needed. Students who use these materials are encouraged to replace what they have used or donate something that they think others could use.

Show Proof That Mastery Matters

After concluding a lesson, identify immediate, specific, and practical ways that students can use the information. For example, give them some math problems based upon something important in their lives. Teenagers love music, so get them to create and use an equation by thinking about the maximum size an entertainment center could be while still leaving enough space in their room for a bed and dresser. During or after studying the explorers, have the students list the common characteristics among the explorers and then have them discuss how similar characteristics might be needed today while exploring new territory or discovering new products. A physics lesson could include concepts such as weight and leverage if students were asked to figure out whether a Nike sneaker with Air Jordan buffers provides more support or leverage than a generic brand. The point is that students are more motivated to learn and make connections when they see how the material relates to their lives.

> **Suggestion.** Try to have each lesson or unit of instruction end with a practical demonstration on how the content relates to the lives of your students. You might even include specific classroom situations or real-life application of the content of your tests. Use real-life material that was discussed in class along with the names of students who had specific points of view when testing for content and concepts.

Focus on Success

Hope is created and sustained in classrooms that emphasize success. Although we cannot make it impossible for students to fail, good teaching requires that we make it extremely difficult for students to fail. This attitude enables us to emphasize success while maintaining high expectations. I remember observing a middle school teacher who expressed excitement when students made mistakes. It was common for him to say such things as, "That is one of the best mistakes I have seen today and this is what it shows. . . ." When he gave back a paper with a failing grade, his message was, "You got 4, 5, and 7 correct, but you missed 2, 3, and 9. Those questions were about area and perimeter, which I am going to review today. If you want to get your grade up, you can do those again. Congratulations on the ones you did well."

> **Suggestion.** Preface a criticism or suggestion for improvement with a comment of approval related to something worthy of notice. As with the example above, this can feel like a stretch, but it is a far more effective way of having students hear what they need to do to improve.

Focus on the Learning Process

When information is shared in brain-friendly ways, more learning occurs (Caine & Caine, 1991; Sylwester, 1995). Teaching processes that affect motivation can be guided by our understanding of multiple intelligences (e.g., Armstrong, 1998; Gardner, 1993), learning styles (Dunn & Dunn, 1982), and preferred learning activities (Goodlad, 1984). Teachers can become their own ongoing researchers with their students in some easy-to-implement ways. Periodic surveys can help. For example, students should be asked the following:

1. Think about something you do or have done in which you are successful.

2. What was it about the situation that helped you succeed? Did other people help? What did they do?

3. What does it take to make you succeed?

4. What kinds of rules or procedures do you need to help you succeed?

It can be helpful to keep a suggestion box in the classroom where students can contribute their ideas and thoughts about how the class can be even more motivational for them. Let students know that you will try to include their ideas and that you may be consulting with them from time to time about their suggestions.

Give Before You Get

Like it or not, good teaching includes good sales techniques. To inspire motivation among our poorly motivated students, we must try to sell them on the idea that working at school and achieving is a good thing. We know from the research on effective sales that getting people to do what you ask is made more effective by first giving them something they value or appreciate. Salespeople send us birthday cards or season's greetings because they know that this creates a certain obligation the next time they call on us. Denis Regan (1971) found in a controlled study that subjects bought more of something they did not need after an unsolicited can of soda was bought for them while they were involved in another activity. Local political organizations know that the way they keep their candidates in office is to make sure they provide a wide range of little favors to the voters. We need to borrow from this research in our efforts to motivate our students.

As educators, we want to influence our students to work and learn. Small favors and appreciation can therefore be very effective tools. Little things can include sending a student a birthday card, writing a positive note to the student or parents, and making students valued helpers.

Suggestion. Think of all the little things people do that make you enjoy being recognized or noticed. Which of these things might some or many of your unmotivated students also enjoy? Think of salespeople you like, admire, or simply go to when you want to buy a product. What characteristics do they have, what do they do, or what have they given to you that makes them attractive? As before, identify which of these behaviors or techniques you might borrow when selling poorly motivated students on the importance of what you teach.

Demand More Than You Really Expect

People generally think they are getting a bargain when they get something that is better than expected. This is the principle of contrast, which affects how we perceive a situation and ultimately how we behave. When two things are presented, if the second one is slightly different from the first, we tend to see it as more different than it actually is. So if the price advertised is $100, but the salesperson offers it for $80, the contrast in price is likely to make you think you are getting a very good deal. But as we know, some merchants will increase a price so that they can have a "sale."

To apply this principle to motivating students, establish expectations that are higher than you expect, and then lower the expectations to reflect what you actually want. This may make students think they are getting a deal. For example, expecting that 10 problems will be turned in for homework when you would be entirely satisfied with 5 enables you to elicit acceptable performance while positively commenting on the 5 problems that a particularly unmotivated student turns in. Expecting that more difficult material be mastered first uses the principle effectively when you next ask for something easier. In other words, start tougher and then ease up.

Make Homework a Bonus

Hassles related to homework can be distressing to students, parents, and teachers. Many homework assignments are boring, repetitive, and often meaningless. Sadly, they seem to be given as much or more for reasons of political correctness (pleasing parents or school boards) than for their educational relevance. Homework should be for practice and should be connected to instruction. Teachers should show they value homework by providing feedback within a day or two of receiving the assignment. Anything less reduces its appeal and then makes it attractive only to the more motivated students who care because of the threat of a reduced grade if they do not do the assignment.

Teaching new concepts should not be the goal of homework. In most instances, homework should be optional because it involves practicing a skill or adding detail to what has already been taught. An exception would be the required practicing of basic reading and writing skills in the early grades (because of their critical importance in overall school success). This homework should require only 15 to 20 minutes per day. Otherwise, educators need to have measures of outcomes so that students can decide whether or not they would benefit from doing homework. Perhaps more frequent short quizzes can be given to assess whether or not students have mastered the material to be practiced for homework. Students who meet a predetermined standard for mastery can continue to have optional homework. Those who fall below the standard can be required to do homework until they demonstrate mastery. Rather than punish students for not doing their homework, perhaps we ought to reward those who do it with something like points in a bank account that can be added to a student's grade or traded for some other more highly desirable activity.

> **Suggestion.** Create two categories for homework. The first represents absolutely essential facts or concepts that must be mastered, and the second is for facts or concepts that are good to know but less essential. Consider making those in the first category required assignments and those in the second category optional. You might establish a reward system such as the one described above for completed assignments in either or both categories.

Encourage and Support Positive Affirmations

Many books and other data show the connection between how we think of ourselves and how we behave. School is difficult for most students, so a positive attitude supported by positive affirmations can give students the mental edge they need to be successful. Illustrations, sayings, and specific sentences can be presented regularly to students for thought and practice. Some of the favorites that I have used and suggested are as follows:

- "I am concentrating and achieving."
- "I am my own person, and I make my own decisions."
- "I can ask questions when I have them because I am confident and smart."
- "I am becoming smarter and smarter."
- "I am making good decisions."
- "I can smile and feel good whenever I want."

Suggestion. There are many inspirational posters that can adorn the classroom walls to provide thought, reflection, and hope. The Successories company has many beautifully illustrated posters with such sayings as "Attitude is a little thing that makes a big difference," and "Unless you try to do something beyond what you have already mastered, you will never grow." Shared stories from inspirational books such as the *Chicken Soup for the Soul* series, followed by reflection or discussion, can also provide needed hope, enthusiasm, and confirmation of an "I can do it" attitude.

Questions for Reflection

1. Remember a former teacher who made you feel special. Picture this person very clearly and see him or her saying and doing those things that made you feel special. Write down what was said and done.

2. Think of one of your students who is not living up to his or her potential. What would it take for you to become the equivalent of your special teacher in this student's life?

3. What obstacles are in the way for you and how might you overcome them?

4. What kind of support do you appreciate getting from others when you are faced with difficult, challenging tasks? Unmotivated students might appreciate getting this kind of support from you if they do not get it already. Picture yourself supporting at least one such student in this way.

Chapter 6

Respecting Power

THE BELIEFS THAT WE HAVE ABOUT OUR OWN COMPETENCE, autonomy, and power influence our motivation. People want desperately to be respected and empowered and will often resort to destructive methods when more reasonable pathways are blocked or perceived as unavailable. A common denominator among those committing school shootings has been the shared perception of being put down and disrespected by fellow students. Some students find power and control in their refusals to work. They are competent and capable, but their need to be in control is so strong that they arrive at what is an extremely self-defeating strategy to exert their independence. Whether for competence, autonomy, or influence, poor work and refusals to participate are protective mechanisms that must be respected and challenged in order to help students make better choices. We must help students learn to influence others and define their independence in ways that are more appropriate and less self-defeating than retreating into either aggression or passive inactivity.

Challenge the Refusals Respectfully

Students who refuse to work frustrate teachers who care because they make us feel like failures. After unsuccessful efforts, it is not unusual for educators to give up and adopt the attitude, "It's up to José—I need to give my attention to the students who care!" Giving up is usually a way that we protect ourselves from a student's continued rejection. But the professional approach must always be to find ways of staying personally connected with the student without taking the inappropriate behavior personally. In the case of students who refuse to work, we have a better chance of inspiring motivation when we let go of our need to shape a student's behavior. It is helpful to identify how the student's behavior is actually positive so that we can be encouraging rather than nagging. For example, most students who refuse to work but who come to class are actually learning much of the information being presented. Their need for power and control prevents them from showing us that learning is happening on a regular basis, thus the lack of homework, papers, and preparedness. Their test scores may suffer as well, although it is not unusual for such students to do quite well on exams. These students are apt to do more of what we want when we respond to the positives they demonstrate (i.e., attending and learning) rather than to the negatives that cause hassle and irritation. For example,

> Kate, I know I hassle you a lot about not doing your work and I'll probably keep doing that because I respect you too much to expect anything less than your best. Most students who won't work are either afraid of failing or are needing to feel in charge. I hope that as you get to know me and this class you'll be brave enough to take a chance. Either way, keep coming and keep learning.

Involve Students in Developing Procedures, Rules, and Consequences

Eccles and Midgely (as cited in Azar, 1996) found that middle school students report fewer opportunities for decision making and lower levels of cognitive involvement than they had in elementary school, despite increased cognitive prowess and a more complex social environment. It is perhaps the decreased flexibility of structure and curriculum as students get older that leads to increased problems with motivation. Involving students in many aspects of school life can sustain enthusiasm. One sensible way to do this is to involve students in developing, reviewing, and modifying classroom rules and possibly consequences. My colleague and frequent coauthor, Rick Curwin, and I have long advocated this for students, and teachers have consistently reported better discipline and motivation in classes where students have a significant role.

There are several proven ways to effectively involve students in rule making (Curwin & Mendler, 1988; Mendler, 1992). The best ways are those that support the educator as the classroom leader. Students can develop rules for the teacher that they believe will help them be successful in class. Another option is for students to develop rules for each other. A third idea is shared collaboration in which the educator shares those classroom values or principles that support learning (e.g., a safe learning environment), and students identify specific rules compatible with each of the values.

Suggestion. Choose methods of student involvement that are based upon your style, philosophy, and comfort level. The motivational key is student involvement. How you do it should best reflect your goals as an educator and your style of instruction.

Defer to Student Power

Much of the time, refusals to work and inappropriate behaviors that challenge the teacher's authority are manifestations of a student's desire to take control of her life. By acting against the norms, these students affirm that they can have influence. A simple but effective method that preserves a student's need for power while eliciting compliance is to let students know what you want by letting them know that they have the power to do what you ask. For example, "Evelyn, we both know that you have the power to use respectful language. Thanks for using it." This two-step process can be applied to virtually any situation. State to the student:

1. "We both know that you have the power to _____."

2. "Thanks for using it."

An extremely effective way to gain compliance is to thank a student for doing the right thing before he or she has actually done it.

Suggestion. Identify behaviors that trouble you and that interfere with student motivation in your class. Think of a student who expresses these behaviors and practice using the above two-step process with the student.

Ask for an Opinion

Students feel respected and are likely to behave in a motivated way when they are asked for their opinion and when there is tangible evidence that their opinion influences classroom events. This can be done by approaching selected students and asking for their academic opinion. For example, Mrs. Farley approaches Harlen, a poorly motivated student, after class and asks whether he thinks the class would prefer to study rocks or minerals. Susan, often a poor achiever, is asked an open-ended opinion question that has no factual answer—for example, "If you were a scientist, which disease do you think you would work hardest to eliminate?" Usually disruptive Luisa is approached for her opinion on ways to encourage more students to follow the rules. Students also can be asked to submit good questions for an upcoming unit test.

Suggestion. Consider the following points.

1. Think of all the academic, behavioral, and personal issues that present themselves in your class.

2. Based on the subject you teach (elementary teachers can do this for many subjects), identify a series of things that need to be learned. When the specific sequence of learning does not make much difference (e.g., kinds of trees), solicit the opinions of some of your poorly motivated students about the order in which these areas should be covered.

3. Identify certain rules that are not working well. In private, ask a frequent rule violator for input about what he thinks can be done to get more students to follow the rules.

Teach a Lesson

Getting students involved in teaching certain lessons or specific aspects of a lesson can be both enlightening and empowering. There are many ways of doing this; for example, less motivated students can be required to teach a class in a way that they believe will be motivating for others. To ensure maximum success, provide structure by assigning a topic, date, and framework for the lesson plan students will develop. The framework is optional and can be offered if the student prefers, or the student can be left to develop his or her own plan. After the lesson, process strengths and challenges as you and the student experienced them. Many students become much more empathic, responsive, and respectful of the teacher following this experience as they realize how difficult teaching can be.

Simile\ comparison using "like" or "as"

examples "My soul has grown deep like the rivers"

"The stillness in the room was like the stillness in the air"

Suggestion. Identify your students who regularly complain about boredom or who act unmotivated. Either individually or in a group, tell them that you would love nothing more than their enthusiastic cooperation and participation in class. Acknowledge that you are at a loss about how to get this from them. Further, let them know that because their lack of participation or perhaps disruptiveness interferes with your teaching and with the learning of others, you want to respect their right to be in charge. Tell them about a few of the upcoming topics that will be covered in class and either assign or have them choose a specific topic that they are to teach in a motivating, enthusiastic way. Establish planning markers along the way (times you will be checking with them to assess their progress in planning) as well as an actual date for teaching. Finally, for those who do not or will not prepare, let them know that you will be happy to teach in their place as long as you can count on their cooperation.

Give Responsibility to Direct and Enforce

Recently, a wonderful fifth-grade teacher with several years of experience was bemoaning the lack of responsibility demonstrated by many of her students. They talked incessantly and listened rarely. Threats of privilege loss, offers of a privilege to be earned if behavioral expectations were met, and a variety of other measures were generally ineffective. This teacher identified the class as very creative at times, often doing a good job in small groups that culminated in a report and teaching to the class. It was suggested that because of their positive response while working on projects, she form subgroups of students who would be responsible for ensuring that procedures were followed correctly. These groups also had the authority to enforce rules by giving reminders and imposing various other simple consequences. The strategy worked like a charm and even gave this teacher an opportunity to process frustration with many of the subgroups who were themselves exasperated while trying to get their classmates to behave. The awareness gained by students of what it is like to be at the receiving end of many minor moments of disrespect helped turn their behavior around.

> **Suggestion.** Identify times of the day when listening or following various procedures is generally poor. If you are a secondary educator, think of a class with which you generally have more problems involving minor (but excessive) misbehavior. Empower groups of three or four students to give whatever directions are required if the learning activity is to be successful. You might even discuss possible consequences or interventions that are available. If they encounter difficulties or frustrations, process these with them and help them understand how their cooperation is necessary when you are asking similar compliance from them. Do not forget to thank them for a job well done. It is

advisable to rotate groups daily, weekly, or according to a schedule that is sensible in your classroom.

Use PEP

When you must correct a student, make every effort to do this with privacy, eye contact, and proximity (PEP). It helps students save face and makes them much more amenable to doing what you have asked them to do. In addition to or instead of using this face-to-face strategy with the student, you can use stick-on notes or index cards to convey your message.

Suggestion. Develop index cards with corrective messages on some and appreciative messages on others. Laminate them and give them to students when situations arise in the classroom that are best handled privately. Laminating implies ownership, so pick them up after the desired result is achieved.

Call Home to Problem-Solve

Calling home and talking with a student about your concerns is one of the most effective ways to elicit cooperation while simultaneously demonstrating respect. There is no audience around, so the influence of peers on behavior is minimized. Taking the time to call also shows the student that you care deeply about what she is doing (or not doing). Realize that this strategy is different from calling the parent of a child to discuss the child's behavior. Although that has a place, calling the student directly empowers both you and the student in an effort to jointly identify a solution that can work for both of you.

Suggestion. Identify students who you consider to be poorly motivated. Call one student each night until each has been called once. Assess the degree to which your call has inspired increased effort. You might wish to call and offer feedback to students who are improving. For those who are not improving, repeat the calling procedure at least three times before deciding whether or not to continue.

Show Students They Already Have What It Takes

A sure-fire way to increase motivation is to use social proof and similarity. The first step is to catch students acting or achieving appropriately. The next step is to get them to attribute their success to the skills they already possess. It is extremely empowering and therefore effective when students realize that they already have what it takes to be successful and that all they have to do is more of the same. For example, in a one-on-one moment say, "Max, you have kept your hands and feet to yourself and remembered to do the right thing for the whole reading lesson today. What have you been doing to be successful?" If the student claims not to know, ask how he was able to remember. The better able a student is to attribute success to his own skills and effort, the more likely that he is to repeat the desirable behavior.

> **Suggestion.** Work to have the student build her own strengths by focusing on times of success or near success. It is very important to use your praise only as a means for the student to notice her own success. The long-term success of this strategy is based on the student's ability to attribute positive behavior to her own thoughts or actions.

Use Short-Term Gain

Behavior modification programs rely on short-term gain to change behavior. Stickers, stars, charts, auctions, pizza parties, and extra privileges have become standard methods of motivation in most classrooms. Although these approaches change behavior fast, the change rarely lasts. Behavior modification is overused in most schools and too often contributes to diminished intrinsic motivation. Approaches that rely heavily upon external incentives unwittingly encourage "what's in it for me" games that lead to bribery. Too many students acquire an expectation of entitlement, believing that they should always get something tangible for what they do.

Still, although we run the risk that tangible rewards (extrinsic incentives) may replace mastery (intrinsic satisfaction), behavior modification does make sense when rapid change is the primary goal. For example, hurtful or chaotic behaviors need to be changed quickly in order to ensure safety and success. Children who hit others may benefit from formal behavior modification systems that motivate them to stop hitting by helping them realize that they have the power to control themselves in the presence of desired incentives. An unmotivated student who will read only for points may discover that reading can actually be enjoyable as an activity in and of itself. The incentive can help a child discover the intrinsic value of the activity so that they begin to do it more on their own. When the stakes are high, any method of motivation that is legal, moral, and ethical becomes educationally sound.

> **Suggestion.** Because all behavior modification programs that rely upon external reinforcement have limited results at best, use them only to change behavior quickly; turn to more responsibility-based methods to sustain the gain. Like a paycheck that is required (we would not work without one) but insufficient, external reinforcement is likely to lead to burnout if it becomes or remains our sole incentive

to work. Students primarily need inner tenacity, pride, and self-respect if they are to sustain and build motivation.

Offer Real Choices

Perhaps the most significant method of motivating is to actually give the power of learning directly to the student. While educators must define the academic standards and basic classroom procedures, students should be encouraged to share their input as much as possible. The more involved students are in choosing aspects of what they learn and how they can best be evaluated, the less need they have to demonstrate power in negative ways. The simplest way to encourage ownership of learning is to offer students significant choices. "Answer three of these six questions." "By the end of the day, your work needs to be completed—would it be best for you to do it now or during recess?" Choices can be included in most assignments, projects, papers, and tests. Research has found that the more you restrict people, the more attractive the object of restriction becomes. If you tell students not to do something, they may be drawn to the forbidden thing. Therefore, it is best to frame requirements as choices with consequences; for example, "Mai-Li, if you are telling me that you are going to be the one to decide to do your work or not, I would have to agree. You are definitely in charge of that choice. So are you going to get to it now or choose recess as your work time? You have complete power to decide."

> **Suggestion**. It is often best to offer procedural choices while defining expected outcomes. Some students fiercely resist being compelled to participate in activities that they believe make them look stupid or ugly. Changing for gym is one such example. Fewer power struggles are had when

students have choices about how to achieve expected outcomes. For example, is it really necessary for an uncoordinated high school junior to play softball? If the goal is to ensure physical fitness, perhaps an alternative activity should be offered. Rigid curricula with inflexible processes are a bad mix in an era when educators have little leverage they can actually rely upon. We all know that chronically unmotivated students are unaffected by threats to call home, lose points from their grade, or face after-school detention. We must try to keep the bigger picture in mind and hold firm while allowing choice within the details.

Questions for Reflection

1. List all the classroom responsibilities you face tomorrow. Put an asterisk next to those that can be done only by you. Assign all others to your students, particularly to those who seek power in inappropriate ways.

2. Very few people really like being told what to do. Nonetheless, we all get and give directions. How do you want expectations or requirements in your personal or work life to be conveyed to you? Are there some people who tell you what to do more effectively than others? What do they say or do? Do they involve you in the decision making and seek your input? Do they treat you in a dignified way? What matters?

3. What practices do you plan to use to involve your students in their own learning and the activities and administration of the classroom?

Chapter 7

Building Relationships

MUCH OF WHAT RICK CURWIN AND I HAVE ADVOCATED for years in our books and articles has essentially been the need to prevent discipline problems by improving our relationships with students and finding ways of preserving these relationships when we need to intervene in student behavior. Motivation is no different. There are simply times when learning is not fun, students cannot understand how it will benefit their lives, and lessons will not be geared to an individual's preferred learning style or intelligence. Learning to remember the times tables can be a painful yet necessary exercise for many students, and one unlikely to be relieved through entertainment.

When my son was an advanced placement physics student greatly challenged by the material, he was actually reassured to hear his teacher advise him and others that they could not yet possibly expect to understand what they were doing because they were still "learning the language" of physics. The teacher assured them that it would begin to make sense later on, and they believed him because he had always been honest and genuine with them. There are times when we inspire motivation because of the work we have previously done to establish trust with our students. It is as if we make deposits into a reservoir of goodwill from which we can make withdrawals when needed. There are times when we must rely on our good relationships to elicit and even inspire optimal effort from our students.

Emphasize and Affirm the Student

Challenging students need us to affirm our belief that they are more important than what they do. They need to know that they are more important to us than their behaviors, even when those behaviors have brought unpleasant consequences. One of our goals should be to make it as hard as we possibly can for students to choose poor behavior or lack of caring. An unmotivated student who persists in being disruptive can be told, for example, "Juanita, I'm embarrassed and disappointed in your behavior. I don't want to look bad in front of everyone and neither do you, so we need to deal with this issue later when we can respect each other's ideas." If the behavior continues, a teacher might say, "Juanita, you'll have to leave class if this doesn't stop. I hope you choose to stay because you are an important member of our class, but if you must leave, come back as soon as you are ready."

While limits and consequences are often needed, difficult students need to know that they are wanted. We must make it as hard as possible for students to reject their education.

Be Open to Student Feedback

Students are more likely to be motivated to learn when their teacher listens to their feedback and makes appropriate accommodations. This is not to be confused with wishy-washy uncertainty. Instead, this should be done in a confident manner by inviting and valuing your students' perceptions and being open to hearing what students think they need in order to succeed.

Suggestion. Seek feedback from your students periodically. Questions like the following can lead to helpful information.

1.   What can I do to be a better teacher for you?

2.   How can I help you be successful?

3.   Two things I say or do that you think I should continue doing are _____.

4.   Two things I say or do that you wish I would do less of are _____.

Send Notes to Students

Asking for what you want can be more effective in the form of a note that is sent to the student either in class or at home. The note should contain something positive followed with concerns or questions. For example,

> Bill, I am really pleased that you did your assignment today. I hope you feel proud. It reminded me that I would like to see that kind of effort more often from you. Tonight's homework is _____. Let me know if there is any help you might need from me to do it well. I'll look forward to seeing your best effort.

You can send notes of appreciation after having corrective feedback conferences with students. This brief and thoughtful response can go a long way toward motivating changed behavior. A handwritten note might include the following sentiments: "Ticia, I appreciate your hearing my feedback today and giving some thought to what we discussed. If you'd like to talk further, let me know. Thanks."

Using humor can also be a helpful strategy. Offering a multiple-choice exercise can add levity and still make the point:

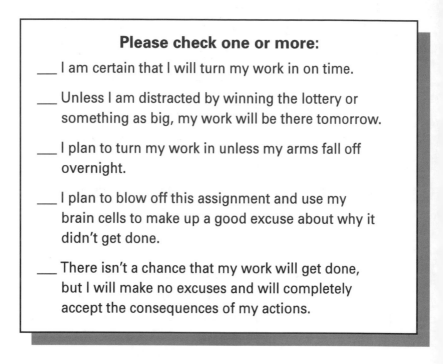

Please check one or more:

___ I am certain that I will turn my work in on time.

___ Unless I am distracted by winning the lottery or something as big, my work will be there tomorrow.

___ I plan to turn my work in unless my arms fall off overnight.

___ I plan to blow off this assignment and use my brain cells to make up a good excuse about why it didn't get done.

___ There isn't a chance that my work will get done, but I will make no excuses and will completely accept the consequences of my actions.

Offer Genuine Compliments

It is so much easier to motivate performance when honest feedback, including strengths, is offered. It is important not to sugarcoat feedback to students because the development of healthy self-esteem is strongly influenced by knowledgeable adults who offer clear and helpful corrections when mistakes are made. It is, however, much more likely that corrective feedback will be accepted when students know that their strengths are affirmed and encouraged. So make a daily effort to compliment some aspect of an unmotivated student's behavior or performance.

Suggestion. You can fill in various incomplete sentences that will help give you structure and serve as a reminder to affirm and encourage students who often do not seem deserving. Possibilities are as follows:

1. I like it when _____.

2. Some days it takes a lot of effort just to show up. Thanks for pushing yourself to come.

3. It helps when you _____.

4. Even though this is not your favorite class, you found a way to _____.

Another way of conveying genuine compliments is to call students at home when you are fairly certain that neither they nor their parent(s) will be there, and leave a complimentary message on the answering machine. It takes very little time and is almost always heard by the student.

Use the 2-Minute Intervention

This is a method that Rick Curwin and I have been teaching educators for many years with very good results. For purposes of increasing effectiveness with an unmotivated student, we advise that you invest 2 uninterrupted, undivided minutes a day for 10 consecutive days with the sole purpose of relationship building. During this time, you are to initiate contact with the student about anything, as long as it meets proper moral and ethical guidelines. The only exception is that you are not allowed to initiate discussion about the student's poor classroom motivation. This is a time when you can get to know the student and the student can get to know you, without either being encumbered by expectations. Initially, the educator and student may experience reluctance and awkwardness. It is for this reason, as well as to establish a pattern of reaching out, that 10 consecutive days is the goal. It is common toward the end of the cycle to see many students begin to behave more acceptably and complete more of their work.

Suggestion. The biggest challenge for many educators is finding an uninterrupted 2-minute interval. Creativity is often needed. One day you might do the 2 minutes during class while the rest of the class is involved in reviewing material or engaged in a cooperative learning activity. Another day you might look for the student at his locker; on yet another day you might "accidentally" drop by the cafeteria while the student is eating. A less intense version of the 2-minute intervention is to occasionally but regularly (weekly or monthly) ask specific students who are not responding favorably within your class, "What is one thing that I can do better for you?" Follow up by asking for one thing that the student can do better for you.

Use Lunch Time to Ask for Behavioral Change

Invite poorly motivated students to have lunch with you occasionally. In fact, you can make this a standard practice to include all students, so that once in a while each student has an opportunity to eat with you. This can be an extremely effective time to give and receive feedback. We have discovered that many difficult students appreciate the special opportunity to eat and share with their teachers.

Host a 5-Minute Focus Group

Before businesses make large investments of time and money, they typically assemble focus groups that provide feedback and information to help them make better decisions. In a similar way, teachers can host their own focus groups by periodically meeting with selected students to find out what is or is not working for them as well as to solicit ideas about how things can improve. Short, biweekly meetings with small groups (five people maximum) are good in most instances.

An educator who is hosting a motivation focus group would convene small groups of students from three categories (very motivated, moderately motivated, and poorly motivated) to get feedback and solicit ideas. Depending upon the goal, students from different motivational categories can be blended for meetings or seen independent of each other. For example, when motivational problems are more group-based, blending students is best. But when students who are unmotivated are "feeding" off each other, you would want to meet with the specific group of identified students for purposes of problem solving. Not only do focus groups provide a way of building relationships, but they are also a nice way of conveying respect and providing a positive empowerment opportunity for your students.

Build a Kindness Train

Lennie Bolinger, a fourth-grade teacher in Dallas, Texas, has her students draw pictures or write kindnesses on 3×5 index cards. Each index card represents the boxcar of a train, so that each time a student catches another doing a kindness and draws or writes about it, the new index card can be attached to the card (kindness) before it. Bolinger's goal is to have kindness spread around the classroom represented by an always-visible train that continually becomes longer and longer. Teachers of older students can easily adapt this by having students share compliments and strengths. Creating a supportive climate is the goal.

Display a Picture of Yourself at the Same Age as Your Students

To connect better with his students, Ted Collins, a seventh-grade teacher in Baltimore, Maryland, brings a few pictures of himself when he was in seventh grade. He blows up the pictures and hangs them in his classroom. When the students ask who the person is, he eventually tells them. His students usually show the same kind of amazement as they do when they see a teacher shopping at the grocery store. There is a sense that he is also a person who was once their age.

Share Stories of Yourself From When You Were a Student

Let students know about you both as an adult and as a younger person. When you see them struggling, take the opportunity to share some of your own similar struggles and how you handle them now or handled them in the past. The reality is that students are trying to figure out how they fit into the world. When a trusted adult takes time to share how he or she handled similar kinds of situations, most students really appreciate it.

Suggestion. You might even share stories about those times and subjects in school that gave you trouble or that you found useless. It can especially help if you put together how something from one or more of these subjects eventually became useful, although it seemed useless when you were taking the class. Pam Shelter, a fifth-grade teacher in San Bernardino, California, responds in a unique way when her students ask "When will I ever use this?" She says, "Write down everything you are going to do for the rest of your life. Give it to me and I'll check off when you'll use it." Naturally, students usually respond by saying that they do not know all the things they will do for the rest of their lives. "That is exactly my point," she says. "There may well be things you'll be doing later in life that you do not know about right now for which this information could be helpful." As indicated earlier in the book, it is best to try connecting the relevance of what we are teaching to how students will use the information, but there are obviously times and situations when making this connection is not possible.

Questions for Reflection

1. When you visit someone's home, what kinds of things do they do to make you feel welcome? How might you do some of these same things in your classroom to make your students feel welcome?

2. When you are unsure of yourself, how do you get helpful encouragement from others? What do they say or do?

3. If all of the staff at your school decided to be welcoming of students, how might that make a difference?

Chapter 8

Expressing Enthusiasm

PHILOSOPHER AND EDUCATOR LEO STEIN was quoted as saying, "the perfect method of learning is analogous to infection. It enters and spreads." Research tells us that our expectations of success for others often influence the degree to which they actually achieve. Simply said, when we expect success, we are more likely to get it. In a similar vein, we can exert strong influence on the behavior of others through the degree of optimism and enthusiasm that we convey. People like being around others who are lively and enthusiastic. At our place of worship, we are likely to be put to sleep or roused to action by the degree of enthusiasm the messenger conveys in the sermon. Most of us enjoy being with people who greet us with warmth and enthusiasm. We enjoy being entertained by musicians who not only play what we want to hear, but play it in ways that create excitement. Our thinking and actions are more likely to be engaged by people who have strong opinions about their positions and who can support their positions with facts that help us understand. In short, the way we convey our subject matter strongly influences how motivated our students are to learn the information.

Let Your Students Know That You Love Being Their Teacher

This is an attitude that needs to be conveyed every day. Let your students know how important they are to you. There are many little ways to let them know—most of the ideas shared in chapter 7, "Building Relationships," apply here as well. Get in the habit of appreciating at least one or two things that happen in class every day. For example, we know that learning is enhanced when the key points of a lesson are summarized. At or toward the end of class, as the lesson is being summarized, share things about the class that warrant appreciation. Use phrases like the following:

- "I was so impressed today when _____."
- "This is really challenging stuff we did today, and I especially appreciate that you _____."
- "I feel like such a lucky teacher to have a class that _____."
- "Wow, the progress I saw today when (name a few students) did _____ is really neat."

Suggestion. Who are the most positive, optimistic, encouraging people you know? What words or phrases do they use naturally? What gestures and other nonverbal cues do they use when expressing these words? Make a list of these verbal and nonverbal behaviors so that you can use some of them to convey support to your students.

Share Your Love of the Subject

Carolyn Sanders, a teacher in Rochester, New York, shared, "I used to think that caring about and loving kids would provide sufficient incentive to make me keep wanting to teach. I learned otherwise when I realized that it was tough to continue liking students who were either aggressive or indifferent." School is primarily about achievement and the mastery of learning. Therefore, while positive relationships with students can often ignite motivation, they are rarely strong enough to sustain it. Loving what you teach is actually a more important tool for motivation than loving your students. Teaching with joy and passion is the one means of motivating that is completely within our control. Students get excited when we are committed to sharing our information in an alive, energetic, excited way.

Be a Lifelong Learner

Students can detect teachers who have taught the same subject in the same way over and over; the material comes across as boring and lifeless. Because learning is about taking risks, show your students that you are a learner. When you are unsure of the answer to a student's question, explore the question in as much depth as possible and when appropriate, let the students know that you will need to learn more about that topic. Be sure to follow up by sharing any new information you found as a result of the research you did. Another way of showing that you are a lifelong learner is to teach some aspect of the same concept differently. For example, use different descriptive examples with different groups when teaching ratios. Keep yourself fresh and stimulated by challenging yourself to keep learning.

> **Suggestion.** Take a class in something outside your current areas of expertise. Allow yourself to feel the uncertainty, insecurity, and excitement involved in learning something new. Realize that we ask students to experience this every day.

Be Lighthearted

Use riddles, jokes, and humor to keep things bouncy in the classroom. Students want to come to classes when teachers make them laugh. Some of us are natural comedians, but most of us are not. Those who aren't search joke books and the comics for help.

Arouse Interest Early

It is virtually impossible to keep things upbeat for a whole day (if you are an elementary educator) or for every class (if you are a secondary educator). So it is strategically best to start each class or interval with a high-interest activity that gets students hooked. This can be a puzzle or riddle that yields a small reward for those who can successfully solve problems within a few minutes. Or you may begin with as many of your jokes as you can so that you can arouse your students' enthusiasm early. Get to the more mundane details in the middle and then finish the lesson with a finale that makes them want to come back for more.

> **Suggestion.** Educators can usually get specific ideas directly from their students about how to arouse their interest. Ask your students to share either verbally or in writing what other teachers have done in the past that made them want to learn or to come to their classes. The answers to your questions can give you ideas that might spark and sustain their motivation. Try, for example, "What kinds of activities get you involved?" or "Tell me three things that you would like to see happen in this class that would make this one of your favorite places to be."

Encourage Drama as a Form of Expressing Knowledge

Research on learning styles, multiple intelligences, and preferred learning activities tells us that there is no one size that fits all when it comes to how students learn, consolidate, and use information. Some learn best by listening, others by looking, and still others by doing. Many learn best when several modalities are combined simultaneously. Dramatic skits that are designed to convey or consolidate information can easily blend multiple modes of learning. Students are involved in the skit while also looking and listening for their roles and those of their classmates.

Be What You Are Teaching

Every so often, you might teach from the perspective of a specific historical figure or book character. Share the essential information with your students in first person. To enhance credibility, dress like the character. When you ask questions, do so as if you were the character.

Use Music

Music can be used as background (while students are working at their desks or in groups), as reinforcement (playing favored tunes after a job well done), or to accompany the teaching of a lesson. The third method uses music from a period in history that relates to a book or to historical events. It is a good way of integrating another learning modality while presenting information.

Use Natural Disasters

Natural disasters provide instant interest and stimulation. Videos of tornadoes, hurricanes, floods, and earthquakes can demonstrate the enormous power that Mother Nature has to wreak havoc and destruction upon us. The wise educator uses these videos as motivational tools by teaching facts and problem-solving skills while using the featured disaster as the main stimulus. Physics lessons can be built around calculating the force needed by a flood to knock down a house of a certain size. Math equations can be used to explore how different elements, when blended together, create a certain outcome. Lessons on how the earth was formed by receding glaciers and raging rivers can be supplemented by showing the new landscape caused by a current flood.

Teach Through Food

Food can be used to teach about historical times, people, or concepts. For example, a unit on colonial America can include foods of that era. As a class, you can prepare and eat these foods. If team teaching is possible, history and home economics can collaborate. Lessons in measurement (math) also become part of the overall scheme. Science becomes involved when children learn about the climates and soils needed to grow the food.

Use Sports

The tremendous status that sports and sports figures have in our culture makes them an excellent motivational tool. Use sports examples in math word problems. Teach percentages by having students calculate batting averages. Use sports publications to inspire reading and reporting. Have students pretend to be sports reporters and assign them to watch a game and then write an exciting review. Encourage them to write an opinion piece about some controversial aspect of a sporting event. For example, after the U.S. Olympic hockey team trashed several hotel rooms in Nagano, Japan, after having been eliminated from competition, nobody on that team took responsibility for the incident. A lesson in character could be blended with problem solving and writing by having students write a column about what happened and what they think should be done about it.

Have Special Theme Days

Like the occasional rearrangement of furniture to give a familiar room a new feel, special theme days can provide a needed change of pace that helps recapture vigor and enthusiasm. Possibilities are

- clash dressing day

- baggy pants day

- look like who you aren't day (e.g., chess club members dress like football players)

- dress like your favorite music group day

- hat day

Questions for Reflection

1. Within your subject or at your grade level, what content do you especially enjoy teaching?

2. We can ignite our enthusiasm for teaching by permitting ourselves to occasionally indulge in doing something just for the fun of it. What have you wanted to do or teach that you would enjoy? What do you fear would happen if you actually did what you wanted?

(continued)

Questions for Reflection (continued)

3. Can you find a way to build at least one fun interval into every teaching period to ensure that you give yourself the joy and enthusiasm you need? You might think of ways to blend sensory-appealing experiences (food, music, drama) into at least one lesson each week.

4. What type of appreciation would you like to get from fellow staff members, parents, or students that would give you energy? Do you give the kind of appreciation you would like to get?

Chapter 9

The Challenge of Changing Lives

ALL EDUCATORS NEED TO BE CONCERNED about those students who become so discouraged that they give up. I hope that the many strategies in this book give you ideas that will make it more difficult for your students to throw in the towel. We certainly compete with so many variables and voices that discourage students and often make them want to give up—unsupportive parents, violence, drugs and alcohol, a cultural attitude of fast and easy, and intense peer pressure.

Our ongoing challenge is to find ways of reconnecting with the natural learner that exists in each of us so that students reawaken with excitement and enthusiasm to the process of learning. Our students need us to have high expectations, apply consequences that teach them when they make mistakes, and affirm who they are. They need us to not give up on them, especially when they are giving up on themselves. We must daily remind ourselves of the enormous influence we can have in changing in our students' lives by awakening them to the many possibilities that a deeper understanding and awareness of the world around them provides.

References

Armstrong, T. (1998). *Awakening genius*. Alexandria, VA: Association for Supervision and Curriculum Development.

Azar, S. (1996). Schools the source of rough transitions. *Monitor on Psychology, 27*(6), 14.

Caine, R. N., & Caine, G. (1991). *Making connections: Teaching and the human brain*. Alexandria, VA: Association for Supervision and Curriculum Development.

Csikszentmihalyi, M. F. (1990). *Flow: The psychology of optimal experience*. New York: Harper Perennial.

Curwin, R. L. (1992). *Rediscovering hope*. Bloomington, IN: National Educational Service.

Curwin, R. L., & Mendler, A. N. (1988). *Discipline with dignity*. Alexandria, VA: Association for Supervision and Curriculum Development.

Dunn, R., & Dunn, K. (1982). *Teaching students through their individual learning styles*. Reston, VA: Reston Publishing Company.

Gardner, H. (1993). *Multiple intelligences: The theory in practice*. New York: Basic Books.

Goodlad, J. I. (1984). *A place called school: Prospects for the future.* San Francisco: McGraw-Hill.

Langer, E. J. (1989). Minding matters. In L. Berkowitz (Ed.), *Advances in experimental social psychology* (vol. 22). New York: Academic Press.

Marzano, R. J. (2000). *Transforming classroom grading.* Arlington, VA: Association for Supervision and Curriculum Development.

Mendler, A. N. (1992). *What do I do when . . . ? How to achieve discipline with dignity in the classroom.* Bloomington, IN: National Educational Service.

Mendler, A. N. (1997). *Power struggles: Successful techniques for educators.* Rochester, NY: Discipline Associates.

Mendler, A. N., & Curwin, R. L. (1998). Seven keys to motivating difficult students. *Reaching Today's Youth, 3*(3), 13–15.

Mendler, A. N., & Curwin, R. L. (1999). *Discipline with dignity for challenging youth.* Bloomington, IN: National Educational Service.

Regan, D. T. (1971). Effects of a favor and liking on compliance. *Journal of Experimental Social Psychology, 7,* 627–639.

Sylwester, R. (1995). *A celebration of neurons: An educator's guide to the human brain.* Alexandria, VA: Association for Supervision and Curriculum Development.

Tomlinson, C. A. (2000). Reconcilable differences? Standards-based teaching and differentiation. *Educational Leadership, 58*(1), 7.

About the Author

ALLEN N. MENDLER, PH.D., is an educator, school psychologist, and the parent of three children. He has worked extensively with children of all ages, with an emphasis on developing effective strategies for educators and youth professionals to help challenging students succeed. As one of the internationally recognized authors of *Discipline with Dignity,* Dr. Mendler has given thousands of workshops throughout the United States and internationally, and is highly acclaimed as a keynote speaker and presenter for numerous educational organizations.

Dr. Mendler is the author or co-author of several books, including *As Tough as Necessary, What Do I Do When . . . ? How to Achieve Discipline with Dignity in the Classroom, Discipline with Dignity for Challenging Youth,* and *Power Struggles: Effective Methods for Educators.* His articles have appeared in many journals, including *Educational Leadership, Parenting,* and *Reaching Today's Youth.* He lives with his family in Rochester, New York.

About *Motivating Students Who Don't Care*
and the National Educational Service

The mission of the National Educational Service is to provide tested and proven resources that help those who work with youth create safe and caring schools, agencies, and communities where all children succeed. *Motivating Students Who Don't Care* is just one of many resources and staff development opportunities NES provides that focus on building a community circle of caring. If you have any questions, comments, articles, manuscripts, or youth art you would like us to consider for publication, please contact us at the address below. Or visit our website at:

www.nesonline.com

Staff Development Opportunities Include:

Improving Schools Through Quality Leadership
Integrating Technology Effectively
Creating Professional Learning Communities
Building Cultural Bridges
Discipline With Dignity
Ensuring Safe Schools
Managing Disruptive Behavior
Reclaiming Youth at Risk
Working With Today's Families

National Educational Service
304 West Kirkwood Avenue, Suite 2
Bloomington, IN 47404-5132
(812) 336-7700
(800) 733-6786 (toll-free number)
FAX (812) 336-7790
e-mail: nes@nesonline.com
www.nesonline.com

NEED MORE COPIES OR ADDITIONAL
RESOURCES ON THIS TOPIC?

Need more copies of this book? Want your own copy? Need additional resources on this topic? If so, you can order additional materials by using this form or by calling us toll free at (800) 733-6786 or (812) 336-7700. Or you can order by FAX at (812) 336-7790, or visit our website at www.nesonline.com.

Title	Price*	Quantity	Total
Motivating Students Who Don't Care	$ 9.95		
Adventure Education for the Classroom Community	89.00		
As Tough as Necessary: Discipline with Dignity (video)	395.00		
Building Successful Partnerships	18.95		
Developing Literacy and Workplace Skills: Teaching for the 21st Century	59.95		
Discipline with Dignity for Challenging Youth	24.95		
Discipline with Dignity (video)	356.00		
Parents Assuring Student Success	24.95		
Power Struggles	11.95		
Teasing and Harassment: The Frames and Scripts Approach for Teachers and Parents	9.95		
		SUBTOTAL	
		SHIPPING	
Continental U.S: Please add 6% of order total. Outside continental U.S.: Please add 8% of order total.			
		HANDLING	
Continental U.S.: Please add $4. Outside continental U.S.: Please add $6			
		TOTAL (U.S. funds)	

*Price subject to change without notice.

❏ Check enclosed   ❏ Purchase order enclosed
❏ Money order   ❏ VISA, MasterCard, Discover, or American Express (circle one)

Credit Card No._____ Exp. Date_____
Cardholder Signature _____

SHIP TO:
First Name_____ Last Name_____
Position _____
Institution Name_____
Address _____
City_____ State_____ ZIP_____
Phone_____ FAX_____
E-mail _____

National Educational Service
304 West Kirkwood Avenue, Suite 2
Bloomington, IN 47404-5132
(812) 336-7700 • (800) 733-6786 (toll-free number)
FAX (812) 336-7790
e-mail: nes@nesonline.com • www.nesonline.com